Quick Ukulele Chords

Simple Search

No-Fuss, Flick-thru Guides

Jake Jackson

Publisher and Creative Director: Nick Wells

Project, design and media integration: Jake Jackson

Website and software: David Neville with Stevens Dumpala and Steve Moulton

Editorial: Gillian Whitaker and Cat Taylor

First published 2022 by
FLAME TREE PUBLISHING
6 Melbray Mews
Fulham, London SW6 3NS
United Kingdom
flametreepublishing.com

Music information site:
flametreemusic.com

26 25 24 23 22
10 9 8 7 6 5 4 3 2 1

ISBN: 978-1-83964-945-5

Printed and bound in the UK by Clays Ltd, Elcograf S.p.A.

The CIP record for this book is available from the British Library.

Android is a trademark of Google Inc. Logic Pro, iPhone and iPad are either registered trademarks or trademarks of Apple Computer Inc. in the United States and/or other countries. Cubase is a registered trademark or trademark of Steinberg Media Technologies GmbH, a wholly owned subsidiary of Yamaha Corporation, in the United States and/or other countries. Nokia's product names are either trademarks or registered trademarks of Nokia. Nokia is a registered trademark of Nokia Corporation in the United States and/or other countries. Samsung and Galaxy are both registered trademarks of Samsung Electronics America, Ltd. in the United States and/or other countries.

Every effort has been made to contact copyright holders. We apologize in advance for any omissions and would be pleased to add appropriate acknowledgement in subsequent editions of this publication.

Jake Jackson is a writer and musician. He has created and contributed to over 20 practical music books, including *Reading Music Made Easy*, *Play Flamenco* and *Piano and Keyboard Chords*. His music is available on iTunes, Amazon and Spotify amongst others.

See & Hear
Web Links

Standard
Tuning

Quick Ukulele Chords

Simple
Search

No-Fuss,
Flick-thru
Guides

Jake Jackson

Flame Tree
Music
CHORDS • SCALES
flametreemusic.com

Contents

The Chords

Online access
flametreemusic.com

Scan the code
to hear the chord

Introduction

Learning to play the ukulele can be fun and rewarding. Playing on your own, with friends, listening and playing along to songs, the ukulele is an easy instrument to pick up and play.

The quickest way to start is to learn some chords. They're the building blocks of all musical compositions so we've tried to make the following pages as straightforward as possible.

The book is organised by key and offers you plenty of information to help you build your understanding. Each chord is clearly laid out, with the musical spelling, and suggested fingering for each string of the instrument.

When you've learned the basics, you can start to practise chord shapes, and moving from one chord to the next. Online there are plenty of sources for music for popular and classic songs.

For a quick start take a look at **C Major**, **D Major**, **G Major** and **E Minor** – these four chords are simple to learn and form the basis of thousands of popular songs. When you've mastered those, try substituting chords with 7ths and 9ths. You'll find that even the complicated-looking chords are helpful when working with other instruments because with only four strings you can quickly bring a different voicing to the overall sound without too much difficulty. Good luck.

Jake Jackson

Online access
flametreemusic.com Scan the code
to hear the chord

Playing the Ukulele

Each step on the fretboard represents a note. Each note up the fretboard is higher than the one it precedes. The difference between each note is called an interval, and these intervals are used to make scales, which in turn are used to make chords.

Playing every note on a piano, from left to right, using all the white and the black keys, is similar to playing every note on every string from bass to treble strings on a guitar. A standard ukulele is slightly different because although every fret represents a different interval, the standard tuning of most ukuleles presents a **G string** that is only two intervals lower than the top, **A string**. This gives the ukulele its unique high-pitched tone and means that the root note of a chord (i.e. the note that gives the chord its name) is often on the 2nd or 3rd string. The notes on the first five frets across the neck are shown on page 9.

Right Hand Techniques

If you listen to a few songs you'll hear the time signatures, usually $\frac{4}{4}$ for rock and pop, or $\frac{3}{4}$ and $\frac{6}{8}$ for other styles such as folk and country. For the ukulele there are two main techniques for the right hand: finger picking and strumming. The fingers offer a wider range of styles, but can be harder to learn at first so many start with strumming which is a compelling percussive technique, suitable for playing along with other instruments.

Online access
flametreemusic.com

Scan the code
to hear the chord

Here are a few strumming patterns to help you get started.

With the **open string notes** at the **top** here are the notes for the first five frets, the **A String** facing down:

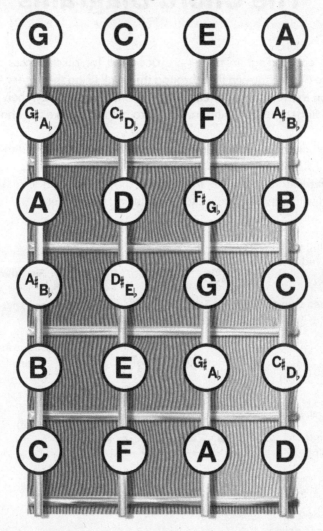

The Chord Diagrams

The chord diagram pages are designed for quick access and ease of use. You can flick through the book using the letters A to G on the top corner of each page to find the right key, then use the finger positions and fretboard to help you make the chord.

Each chord is provided with a Chord Spelling underneath the chord diagram, and will help you check each note. It's also a great way to learn the structure of the sounds you're making and will help with melodies and playing with others.

String isn't played

Open string note

String facing up

QR code link to hear the chord online

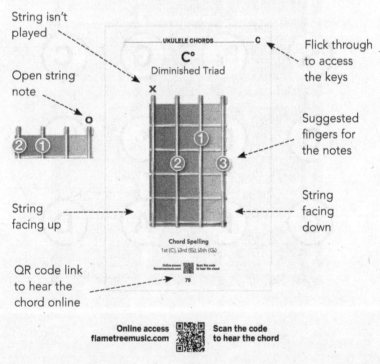

UKULELE CHORDS — C

C°
Diminished Triad

Flick through to access the keys

Suggested fingers for the notes

String facing down

Chord Spelling
1st (C), ♭3rd (E♭), ♭5th (G♭)

Online access
flametreemusic.com

Scan the code
to hear the chord

79

Online access
flametreemusic.com

Scan the code
to hear the chord

Tuning the Ukulele: The open strings on a ukulele work in a different way to a guitar: the G string is just two notes lower than the A string. This gives the characteristic jangling sound. Here are the same notes on a piano, in order of their pitch. **Middle C** is **bold.**

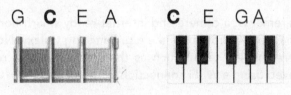

G **C** E A   **C** E G A

Fingerings: ❶ is the index finger   ❷ is the middle finger
                   ❸ is the ring finger   ❹ is the little finger

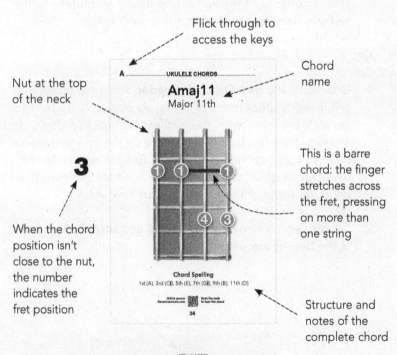

Flick through to access the keys

Chord name

Nut at the top of the neck

A ———— UKULELE CHORDS ————

Amaj11
Major 11th

3

This is a barre chord: the finger stretches across the fret, pressing on more than one string

When the chord position isn't close to the nut, the number indicates the fret position

Chord Spelling
1st (A), 3rd (C♯), 5th (E), 7th (G♯), 9th (B), 11th (D)

Online access
flametreemusic.com

Scan the code to hear the chord

34

Structure and notes of the complete chord

The Audio Links

Requirements: a camera and internet-ready smartphone (e.g. iPhone, any Android phone – e.g. Samsung Galaxy, Nokia) or camera-enabled tablet such as the iPad). The best result is achieved using a Wi-Fi connection.

Either:

1. Point your camera at the QR code. Most modern smartphones read the link automatically and offer you the website **flametreemusic.com** to connect online.

Or:

1. Download any **free QR code reader**. An app store search will reveal a great many of these, so obviously it's best to go with the ones with the highest ratings and don't be afraid to try a few before you settle on the one that works best for you. Tapmedia's QR Code Reader app, Kaspersky QR Scanner or QR Code Reader by Scan are perfectly fine, although some of the free apps also have ads.

2. On your smartphone, open the app and **scan** the **QR code** at the base of any particular page.

Online access
flametreemusic.com

Scan the code
to hear the chord

Then:

3. Scanning the chord will bring you to the chord page. From there you can access and **hear** the complete library of scales and chords on **flametreemusic.com**.

   On pages where QR codes feature alongside particular chords and scales, those codes will take you directly to the relevant chord or scale on the website.

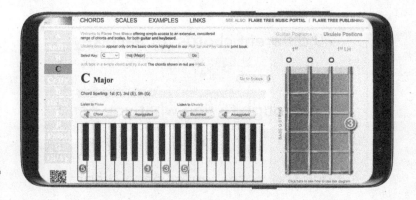

4. Use the drop-down menu to choose from **20 scales** or 12 **free chords** (50 with subscription) per key.

5. Click the sounds! Both piano and guitar audio is provided. This is particularly helpful when you're playing with others.

   The QR codes give you direct access to chords and scales. You can access a much wider range of chords if you register.

Online access
flametreemusic.com

Scan the code
to hear the chord

Easy Access

Organized from A to G keys

•

20 different chords for each key

•

Flick through to find what you need

•

Check the notes under each diagram

•

Use the QR code to hear the chord

•

Online access
flametreemusic.com Scan the code
to hear the chord

Quick Ukulele Chords

Simple Search

No-Fuss, Flick-thru Guides

Online access
flametreemusic.com

Scan the code
to hear the chord

A
Major

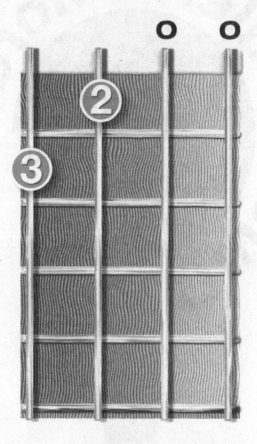

Chord Spelling
1st (A), 3rd (C#), 5th (E)

Am
Minor

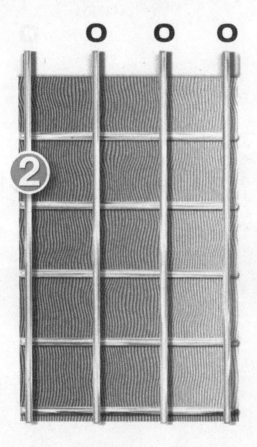

Chord Spelling
1st (A), ♭3rd (C), 5th (E)

Online access
flametreemusic.com

Scan the code
to hear the chord

A+
Augmented Triad

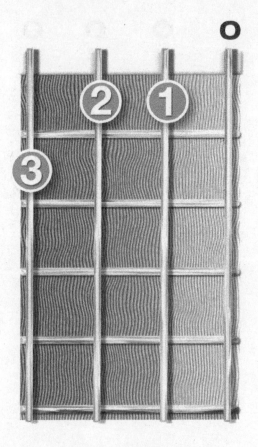

Chord Spelling
1st (A), 3rd (C#), #5th (E#)

Online access
flametreemusic.com

Scan the code
to hear the chord

A°
Diminished Triad

Chord Spelling

1st (A), ♭3rd (C), ♭5th (E♭)

Asus2
Suspended 2nd

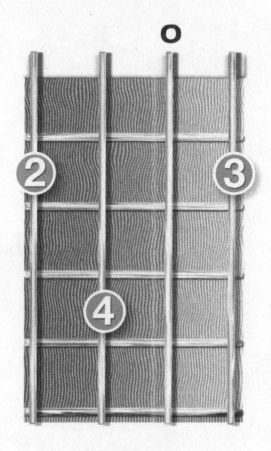

Chord Spelling
1st (A), 2nd (B), 5th (E)

Online access
flametreemusic.com

Scan the code
to hear the chord

Asus4
Suspended 4th

Chord Spelling
1st (A), 4th (D), 5th (E)

Online access
flametreemusic.com

Scan the code
to hear the chord

A5
5th (Power Chord)

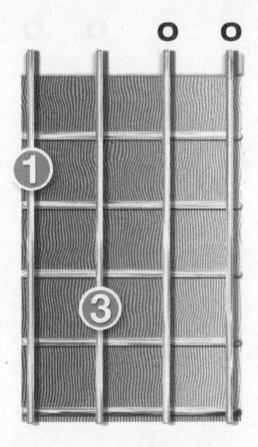

Chord Spelling
1st (A), 5th (E)

Online access
flametreemusic.com Scan the code
to hear the chord

22

A6
Major 6th

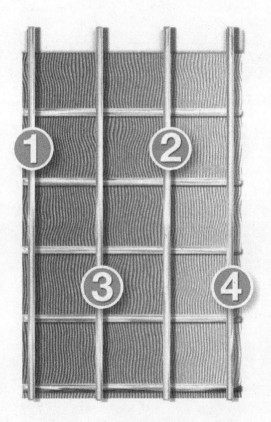

Chord Spelling
1st (A), 3rd (C#), 5th (E), 6th (F#)

Online access
flametreemusic.com

Scan the code
to hear the chord

Am6
Minor 6th

Chord Spelling
1st (A), ♭3rd (C), 5th (E), 6th (F♯)

Online access
flametreemusic.com Scan the code
to hear the chord

A6sus4
6th Suspended 4th

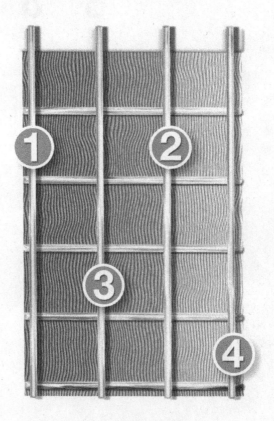

Chord Spelling
1st (A), 4th (D), 5th (E), 6th (F#)

Online access
flametreemusic.com

Scan the code
to hear the chord

Amaj7
Major 7th

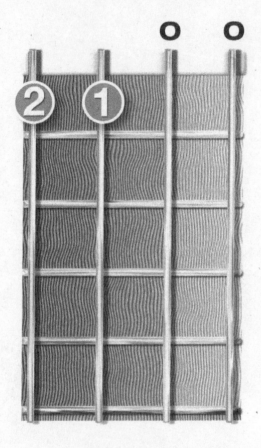

Chord Spelling
1st (A), 3rd (C♯), 5th (E), 7th (G♯)

Online access
flametreemusic.com

Scan the code
to hear the chord

Am7
Minor 7th

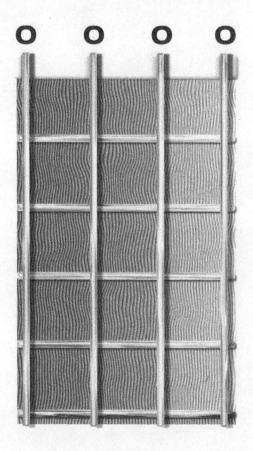

Chord Spelling
1st (A), ♭3rd (C), 5th (E), ♭7th (G)

Online access
flametreemusic.com Scan the code
to hear the chord

A7
Dominant 7th

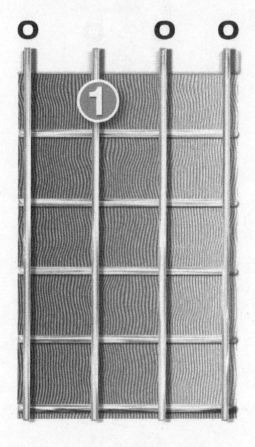

Chord Spelling
1st (A), 3rd (C#), 5th (E), ♭7th (G)

Online access
flametreemusic.com

Scan the code
to hear the chord

A°7
Diminished 7th

Chord Spelling
1st (A), ♭3rd (C), ♭5th (E♭), ♭♭7th (G♭)

Online access
flametreemusic.com Scan the code
to hear the chord

A7sus4
Dominant 7th Suspended 4th

Chord Spelling
1st (A), 4th (D), 5th (E), ♭7th (G)

Amaj9
Major 9th

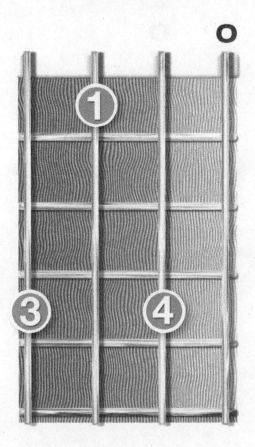

Chord Spelling
1st (A), 3rd (C♯), 5th (E), 7th (G♯), 9th (B)

Online access
flametreemusic.com

Scan the code
to hear the chord

Am9
Minor 9th

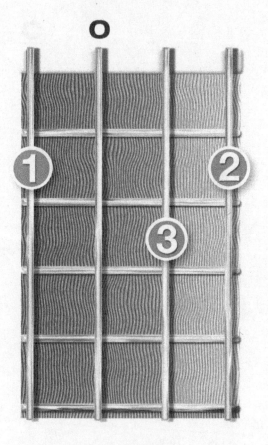

Chord Spelling
1st (A), ♭3rd (C), 5th (E), ♭7th (G), 9th (B)

A9
Dominant 9th

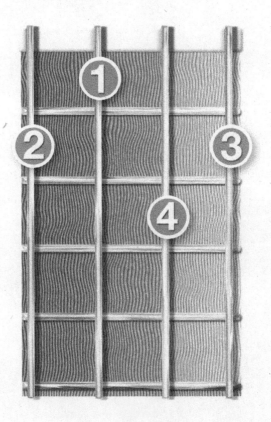

Chord Spelling
1st (A), 3rd (C♯), 5th (E), ♭7th (G), 9th (B)

Online access
flametreemusic.com

Scan the code
to hear the chord

Amaj11
Major 11th

Chord Spelling

1st (A), 3rd (C♯), 5th (E), 7th (G♯), 9th (B), 11th (D)

Amaj13
Major 13th

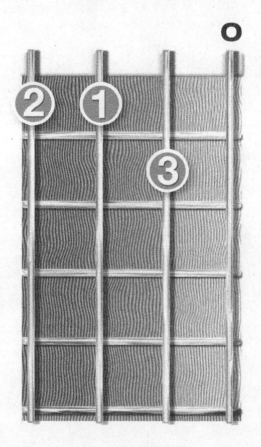

Chord Spelling

1st (A), 3rd (C♯), 5th (E), 7th (G♯), 9th (B), 11th (D), 13th (F♯)

Online access
flametreemusic.com

Scan the code
to hear the chord

A♯/B♭
Major

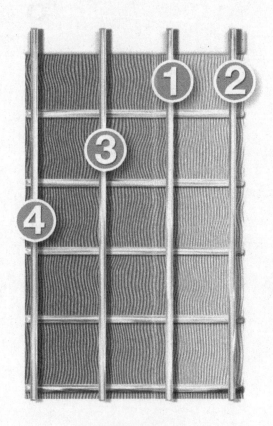

Chord Spelling
1st (B♭), 3rd (D), 5th (F)

A♯/B♭m
Minor

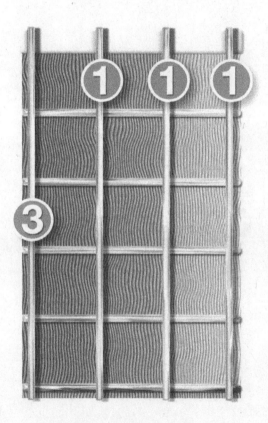

Chord Spelling
1st (B♭), ♭3rd (D♭), 5th (F)

Online access
flametreemusic.com Scan the code
to hear the chord

A#/B♭+
Augmented Triad

Chord Spelling
1st (B♭), 3rd (D), #5th (F#)

Online access
flametreemusic.com

Scan the code
to hear the chord

A♯/B♭°
Diminished Triad

Chord Spelling
1st (B♭), ♭3rd (D♭), ♭5th (F♭)

Online access
flametreemusic.com

Scan the code
to hear the chord

A♯/B♭sus2
Suspended 2nd

Chord Spelling
1st (B♭), 2nd (C), 5th (F)

Online access
flametreemusic.com

Scan the code
to hear the chord

A♯/B♭sus4
Suspended 4th

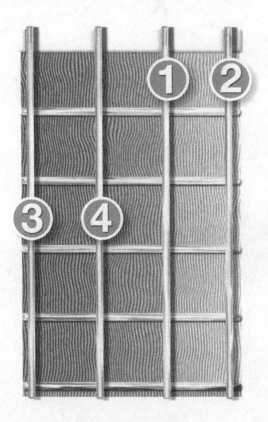

Chord Spelling
1st (B♭), 4th (E♭), 5th (F)

Online access
flametreemusic.com

Scan the code
to hear the chord

A♯/B♭5
5th (Power Chord)

Chord Spelling

1st (B♭), 5th (F)

Online access
flametreemusic.com

Scan the code
to hear the chord

A#/B♭6
Major 6th

Chord Spelling

1st (B♭), 3rd (D), 5th (F), 6th (G)

A♯/B♭m6
Minor 6th

Chord Spelling
1st (B♭), ♭3rd (D♭), 5th (F), 6th (G)

Online access
flametreemusic.com

Scan the code
to hear the chord

A♯/B♭6sus4
6th Suspended 4th

Chord Spelling
1st (B♭), 4th (E♭), 5th (F), 6th (G)

A♯/B♭maj7
Major 7th

Chord Spelling

1st (B♭), 3rd (D), 5th (F), 7th (A)

A♯/B♭m7
Minor 7th

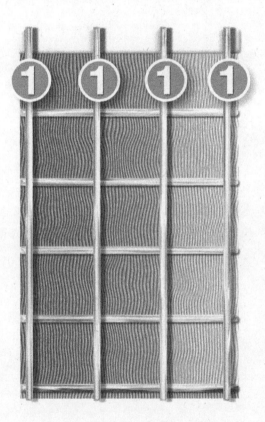

Chord Spelling

1st (B♭), ♭3rd (D♭), 5th (F), ♭7th (A♭)

A♯/B♭7
Dominant 7th

Chord Spelling

1st (B♭), 3rd (D), 5th (F), ♭7th (A♭)

A♯/B♭°7
Diminished 7th

Chord Spelling
1st (B♭), ♭3rd (D♭), ♭5th (F♭), ♭♭7th (A♭♭)

A♯/B♭7sus4
Dominant 7th Suspended 4th

Chord Spelling
1st (B♭), 4th (E♭), 5th (F), ♭7th (A♭)

Online access
flametreemusic.com

Scan the code
to hear the chord

A♯/B♭maj9
Major 9th

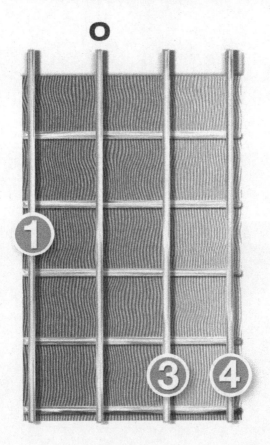

Chord Spelling

1st (B♭), 3rd (D), 5th (F), 7th (A), 9th (C)

Online access
flametreemusic.com

Scan the code
to hear the chord

A#/B♭m9
Minor 9th

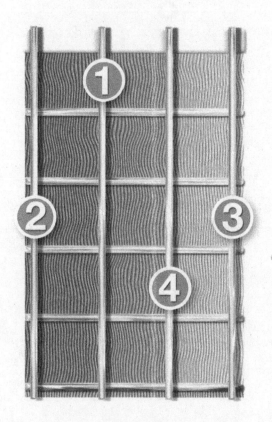

Chord Spelling

1st (B♭), ♭3rd (D♭), 5th (F), ♭7th (A♭), 9th (C)

A♯/B♭9
Dominant 9th

Chord Spelling
1st (B♭), 3rd (D), 5th (F), ♭7th (A♭), 9th (C)

Online access
flametreemusic.com

Scan the code
to hear the chord

A#/B♭maj11
Major 11th

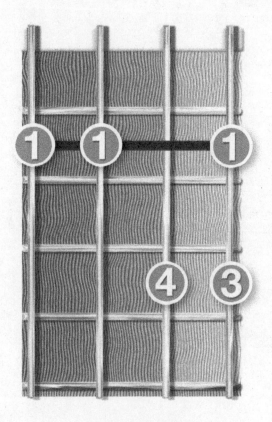

Chord Spelling
1st (B♭), 3rd (D), 5th (F), 7th (A), 9th (C), 11th (E♭)

A♯/B♭maj13
Major 13th

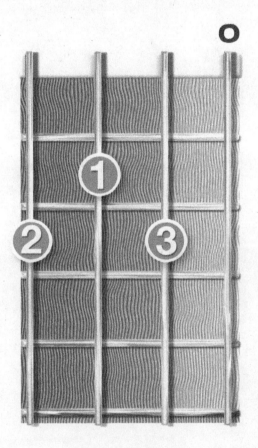

Chord Spelling
1st (B♭), 3rd (D), 5th (F), 7th (A), 9th (C), 11th (E♭), 13th (G)

Online access
flametreemusic.com

Scan the code
to hear the chord

B
Major

Chord Spelling

1st (B), 3rd (D♯), 5th (F♯)

Bm
Minor

Chord Spelling

1st (B), ♭3rd (D), 5th (F♯)

B+
Augmented Triad

Chord Spelling
1st (B), 3rd (D♯), ♯5th (Fx)

Online access
flametreemusic.com Scan the code
to hear the chord

B°
Diminished Triad

Chord Spelling
1st (B), ♭3rd (D), ♭5th (F)

Bsus2
Suspended 2nd

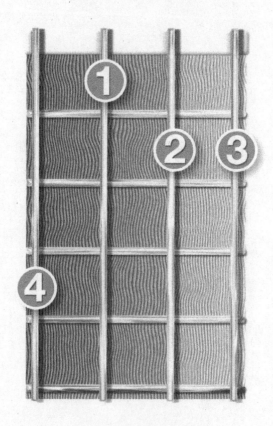

Chord Spelling
1st (B), 2nd (C#), 5th (F#)

Bsus4
Suspended 4th

Chord Spelling
1st (B), 4th (E), 5th (F#)

Online access
flametreemusic.com

Scan the code
to hear the chord

B5
5th (Power Chord)

X   X

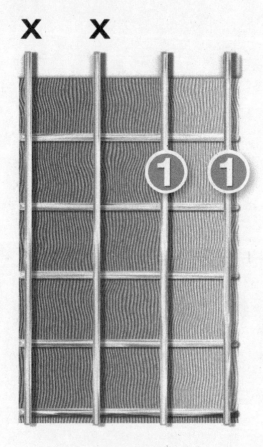

Chord Spelling
1st (B), 5th (F#)

Online access
flametreemusic.com

Scan the code
to hear the chord

B6
Major 6th

Chord Spelling
1st (B), 3rd (D♯), 5th (F♯), 6th (G♯)

Online access
flametreemusic.com

Scan the code
to hear the chord

Bm6
Minor 6th

Chord Spelling

1st (B), ♭3rd (D), 5th (F♯), 6th (G♯)

Online access
flametreemusic.com Scan the code
to hear the chord

B6sus4
6th Suspended 4th

Chord Spelling
1st (B), 4th (E), 5th (F#), 6th (G#)

Online access
flametreemusic.com

Scan the code
to hear the chord

Bmaj7
Major 7th

Chord Spelling

1st (B), 3rd (D#), 5th (F#), 7th (A#)

Bm7
Minor 7th

Chord Spelling

1st (B), ♭3rd (D), 5th (F♯), ♭7th (A)

Online access
flametreemusic.com

Scan the code
to hear the chord

B7
Dominant 7th

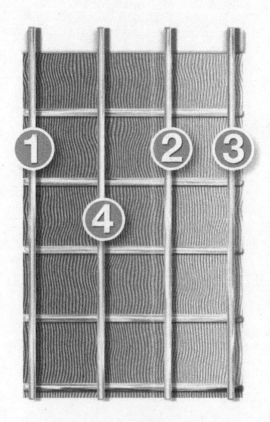

Chord Spelling
1st (B), 3rd (D♯), 5th (F♯), ♭7th (A)

Online access
flametreemusic.com Scan the code
to hear the chord

B°7
Diminished 7th

Chord Spelling
1st (B), ♭3rd (D), ♭5th (F), ♭♭7th (A♭)

B7sus4
Dominant 7th Suspended 4th

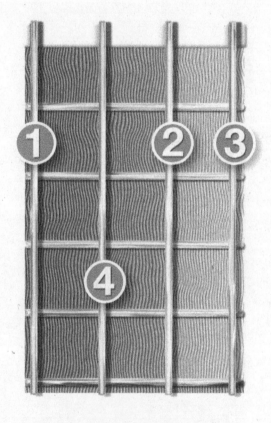

Chord Spelling
1st (B), 4th (E), 5th (F♯), ♭7th (A)

Bmaj9
Major 9th

3

Chord Spelling
1st (B), 3rd (D#), 5th (F#), 7th (A#), 9th (C#)

Online access
flametreemusic.com

Scan the code
to hear the chord

Bm9
Minor 9th

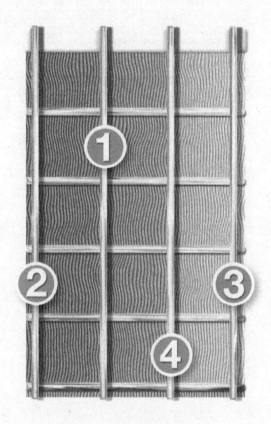

Chord Spelling
1st (B), ♭3rd (D), 5th (F♯), ♭7th (A), 9th (C♯)

Online access
flametreemusic.com

Scan the code
to hear the chord

B9
Dominant 9th

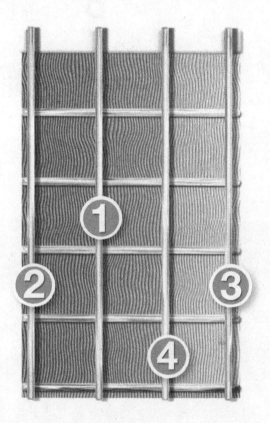

Chord Spelling

1st (B♭), 3rd (D), 5th (F), ♭7th (A♭), 9th (C)

Bmaj11
Major 11th

Chord Spelling
1st (B), 3rd (D♯), 5th (F♯), 7th (A♯), 9th (C♯), 11th (E)

Bmaj13
Major 13th

Chord Spelling

1st (B), 3rd (D♯), 5th (F♯), 7th (A♯), 9th (C♯), 11th (E), 13th (G♯)

Online access
flametreemusic.com

Scan the code
to hear the chord

C
Major

Chord Spelling
1st (C), 3rd (E), 5th (G)

Online access
flametreemusic.com

Scan the code
to hear the chord

Cm
Minor

Chord Spelling

1st (C), ♭3rd (E♭), 5th (G)

Online access
flametreemusic.com

Scan the code
to hear the chord

C+
Augmented Triad

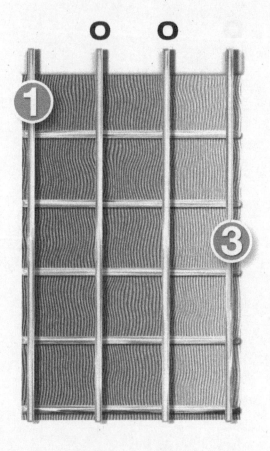

Chord Spelling
1st (C), 3rd (E), #5th (G#)

Online access
flametreemusic.com

Scan the code
to hear the chord

C°
Diminished Triad

Chord Spelling
1st (C), ♭3rd (E♭), ♭5th (G♭)

Online access
flametreemusic.com

Scan the code
to hear the chord

Csus2
Suspended 2nd

Chord Spelling
1st (C), 2nd (D), 5th (G)

Online access
flametreemusic.com

Scan the code
to hear the chord

Csus4
Suspended 4th

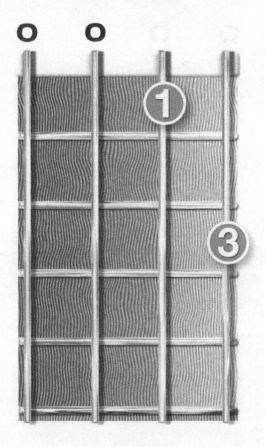

Chord Spelling
1st (C), 4th (F), 5th (G)

Online access
flametreemusic.com

Scan the code
to hear the chord

C5
5th (Power Chord)

Chord Spelling
1st (C), 5th (G)

C6
Major 6th

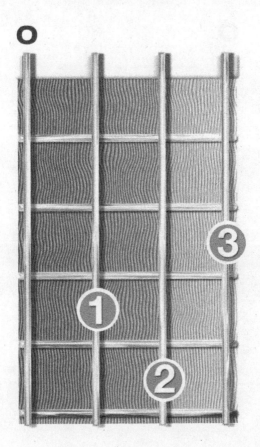

Chord Spelling
1st (C), 3rd (E), 5th (G), 6th (A)

Online access
flametreemusic.com

Scan the code
to hear the chord

Cm6
Minor 6th

Chord Spelling
1st (C), ♭3rd (E♭), 5th (G), 6th (A)

Online access
flametreemusic.com

Scan the code
to hear the chord

C6sus4
6th Suspended 4th

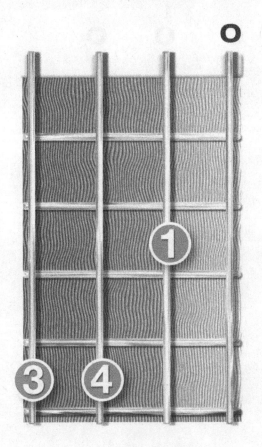

Chord Spelling
1st (C), 4th (F), 5th (G), 6th (A)

Online access
flametreemusic.com Scan the code
to hear the chord

Cmaj7
Major 7th

Chord Spelling
1st (C), 3rd (E), 5th (G), 7th (B)

Online access
flametreemusic.com

Scan the code
to hear the chord

Cm7
Minor 7th

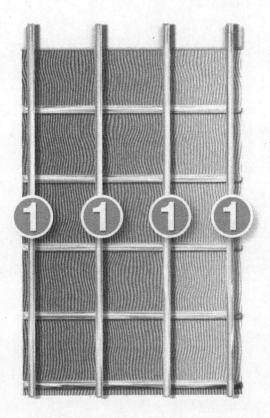

Chord Spelling
1st (C), ♭3rd (E♭), 5th (G), ♭7th (B♭)

Online access
flametreemusic.com Scan the code
to hear the chord

C7
Dominant 7th

Chord Spelling

1st (C), 3rd (E), 5th (G), ♭7th (B♭)

Online access
flametreemusic.com

Scan the code
to hear the chord

C°7
Diminished 7th

Chord Spelling
1st (C), ♭3rd (E♭), ♭5th (G♭), ♭♭7th (B♭♭)

Online access
flametreemusic.com

Scan the code
to hear the chord

C7sus4
Dominant 7th Suspended 4th

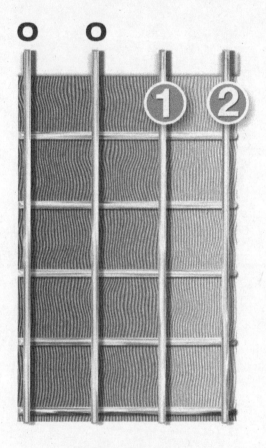

Chord Spelling
1st (C), 4th (F), 5th (G), ♭7th (B♭)

Cmaj9
Major 9th

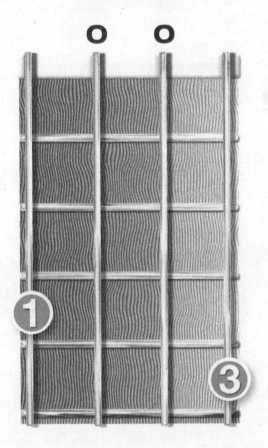

Chord Spelling
1st (C), 3rd (E), 5th (G), 7th (B), 9th (D)

Online access
flametreemusic.com

Scan the code
to hear the chord

Cm9
Minor 9th

2

Chord Spelling
1st (C), ♭3rd (E♭), 5th (G), ♭7th (B♭), 9th (D)

Online access
flametreemusic.com

Scan the code
to hear the chord

C9
Dominant 9th

Chord Spelling
1st (C), 3rd (E), 5th (G), ♭7th (B♭), 9th (D)

Online access
flametreemusic.com Scan the code
to hear the chord

Cmaj11
Major 11th

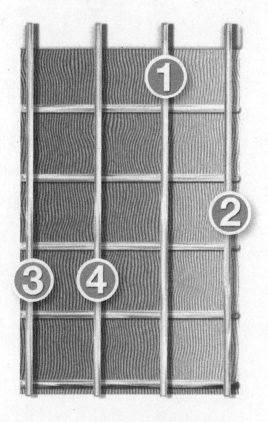

Chord Spelling
1st (C), 3rd (E), 5th (G), 7th (B), 9th (D), 11th (F)

Cmaj13
Major 13th

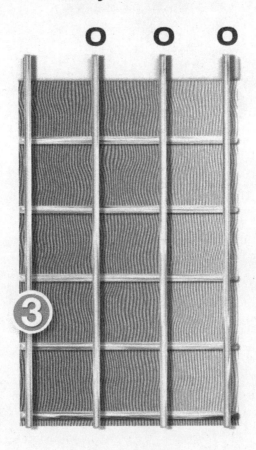

Chord Spelling

1st (C), 3rd (E), 5th (G), 7th (B), 9th (D), 11th (F), 13th (A)

Online access
flametreemusic.com

Scan the code
to hear the chord

C#/Db
Major

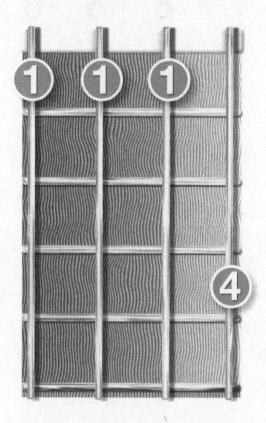

Chord Spelling
1st (C#), 3rd (E#), 5th (G#)

Online access
flametreemusic.com

Scan the code
to hear the chord

C♯/D♭m
Minor

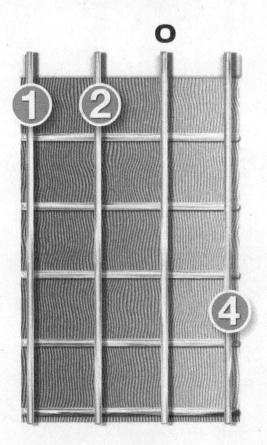

Chord Spelling
1st (C♯), ♭3rd (E), 5th (G♯)

C♯/D♭+
Augmented Triad

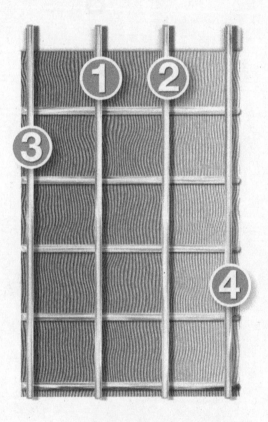

Chord Spelling

1st (C♯), 3rd (E♯), ♯5th (Gx)

Online access
flametreemusic.com

Scan the code
to hear the chord

C#/D♭°
Diminished Triad

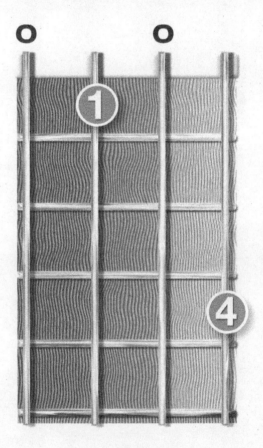

Chord Spelling

1st (C#), ♭3rd (E), ♭5th (G)

C#/D♭sus2
Suspended 2nd

Chord Spelling
1st (C#), 2nd (D#), 5th (G#)

C#/D♭sus4
Suspended 4th

Chord Spelling
1st (C#), 4th (F#), 5th (G#)

Online access
flametreemusic.com

Scan the code
to hear the chord

C#/D♭5
5th (Power Chord)

Chord Spelling
1st (C#), 5th (G#)

C♯/D♭6
Major 6th

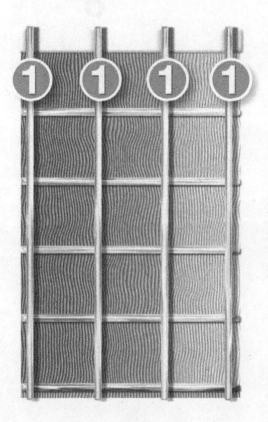

Chord Spelling

1st (C♯), 3rd (E♯), 5th (G♯), 6th (A♯)

Online access
flametreemusic.com Scan the code
to hear the chord

C#/D♭m6
Minor 6th

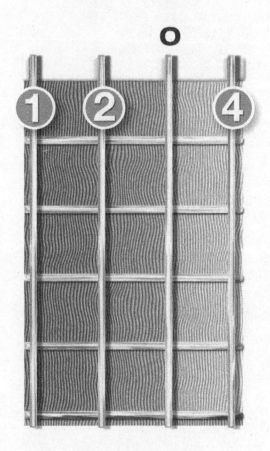

Chord Spelling
1st (C#), ♭3rd (E), 5th (G#), 6th (A#)

C#/Db6sus4
6th Suspended 4th

Chord Spelling
1st (C#), 4th (F#), 5th (G#), 6th (A#)

Online access
flametreemusic.com

Scan the code
to hear the chord

C#/D♭maj7
Major 7th

Chord Spelling
1st (C#), 3rd (E#), 5th (G#), 7th (B#)

Online access
flametreemusic.com

Scan the code
to hear the chord

C#/D♭m7
Minor 7th

Chord Spelling
1st (C#), ♭3rd (E), 5th (G#), ♭7th (B)

C#/D♭7
Dominant 7th

Chord Spelling
1st (C#), 3rd (E#), 5th (G#), ♭7th (B)

C♯/D♭°7
Diminished 7th

Chord Spelling

1st (C♯), ♭3rd (E), ♭5th (G), ♭♭7th (B♭)

Online access
flametreemusic.com

Scan the code
to hear the chord

C#/D♭7sus4
Dominant 7th Suspended 4th

Chord Spelling
1st (C#), 4th (F#), 5th (G#), ♭7th (B)

C#/D♭maj9
Major 9th

5

Chord Spelling
1st (C#), 3rd (E#), 5th (G#), 7th (B#), 9th (D#)

Online access
flametreemusic.com

Scan the code
to hear the chord

C♯/D♭m9
Minor 9th

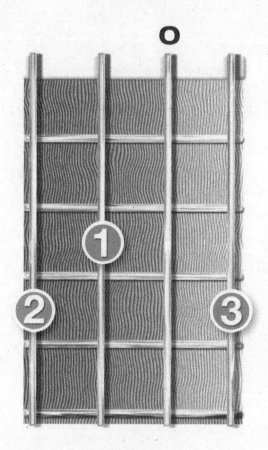

Chord Spelling
1st (C♯), ♭3rd (E), 5th (G♯), ♭7th (B), 9th (D♯)

Online access
flametreemusic.com

Scan the code
to hear the chord

C♯/D♭9
Dominant 9th

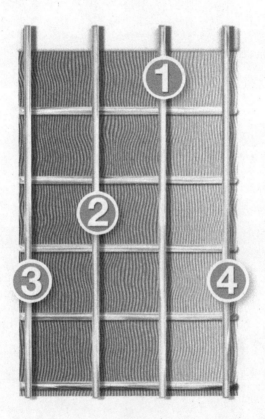

Chord Spelling
1st (C♯), 3rd (E♯), 5th (G♯), ♭7th (B), 9th (D♯)

Online access
flametreemusic.com

Scan the code
to hear the chord

C#/D♭maj11
Major 11th

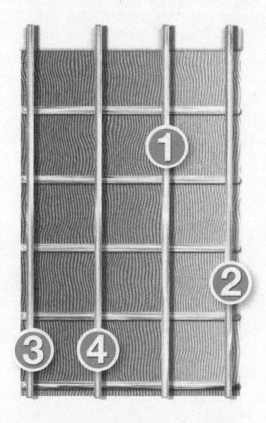

Chord Spelling

1st (C#), 3rd (E#), 5th (G#), 7th (B#), 9th (D#), 11th (F#)

Online access
flametreemusic.com

Scan the code
to hear the chord

C#/D♭maj13
Major 13th

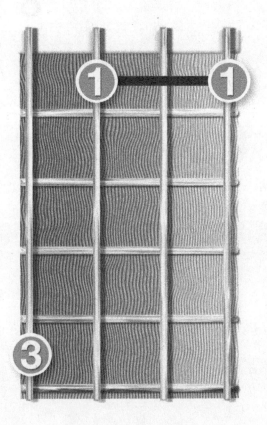

Chord Spelling

1st (C#), 3rd (E#), 5th (G#), 7th (B#), 9th (D#), 11th (F#), 13th (A#)

Online access
flametreemusic.com

Scan the code
to hear the chord

D
Major

Chord Spelling
1st (D), 3rd (F♯), 5th (A)

Online access
flametreemusic.com

Scan the code
to hear the chord

Dm
Minor

Chord Spelling
1st (D), ♭3rd (F), 5th (A)

Online access
flametreemusic.com

Scan the code
to hear the chord

D+
Augmented Triad

Chord Spelling
1st (D), 3rd (F#), #5th (A#)

D°
Diminished Triad

Chord Spelling

1st (D), ♭3rd (F), ♭5th (A♭)

Online access
flametreemusic.com

Scan the code
to hear the chord

Dsus2
Suspended 2nd

Chord Spelling
1st (D), 2nd (E), 5th (A)

Dsus4
Suspended 4th

Chord Spelling
1st (D), 4th (G), 5th (A)

Online access
flametreemusic.com

Scan the code
to hear the chord

D5
5th (Power Chord)

Chord Spelling
1st (D), 5th (A)

Online access
flametreemusic.com

Scan the code
to hear the chord

D6
Major 6th

Chord Spelling

1st (D), 3rd (F#), 5th (A), 6th (B)

Online access
flametreemusic.com

Scan the code
to hear the chord

Dm6
Minor 6th

Chord Spelling
1st (D), ♭3rd (F), 5th (A), 6th (B)

D6sus4
6th Suspended 4th

Chord Spelling

1st (D), 4th (G), 5th (A), 6th (B)

Dmaj7
Major 7th

Chord Spelling
1st (D), 3rd (F♯), 5th (A), 7th (C♯)

Online access
flametreemusic.com

Scan the code
to hear the chord

Dm7
Minor 7th

Chord Spelling

1st (D), ♭3rd (F), 5th (A), ♭7th (C)

Online access
flametreemusic.com

Scan the code
to hear the chord

D7
Dominant 7th

Chord Spelling
1st (D), 3rd (F♯), 5th (A), ♭7th (C)

D°7
Diminished 7th

Chord Spelling
1st (D), ♭3rd (F), ♭5th (A♭), ♭♭7th (B)

Online access
flametreemusic.com

Scan the code
to hear the chord

D7sus4
Dominant 7th Suspended 4th

Chord Spelling
1st (D), 4th (G), 5th (A), ♭7th (C)

Online access
flametreemusic.com

Scan the code
to hear the chord

Dmaj9
Major 9th

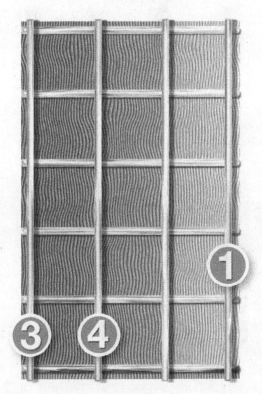

Chord Spelling

1st (D), 3rd (F#), 5th (A), 7th (C#), 9th (E)

Online access
flametreemusic.com

Scan the code
to hear the chord

Dm9
Minor 9th

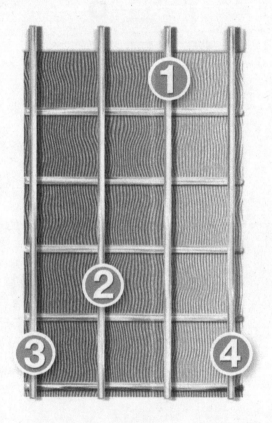

Chord Spelling
1st (D), ♭3rd (F), 5th (A), ♭7th (C), 9th (E)

Online access
flametreemusic.com

Scan the code
to hear the chord

D9
Dominant 9th

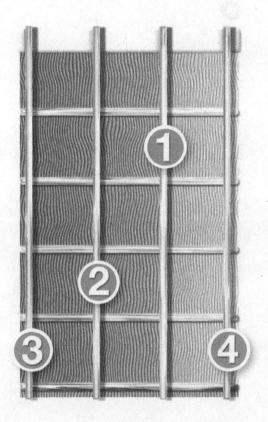

Chord Spelling
1st (D), 3rd (F#), 5th (A), ♭7th (C), 9th (E)

Online access
flametreemusic.com

Scan the code
to hear the chord

Dmaj11
Major 11th

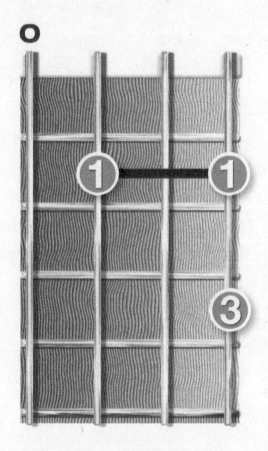

Chord Spelling
1st (D), 3rd (F#), 5th (A), 7th (C#), 9th (E), 11th (G)

Dmaj13
Major 13th

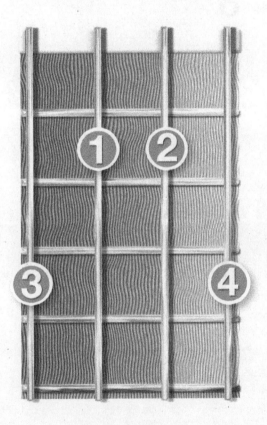

Chord Spelling

1st (D), 3rd (F#), 5th (A), 7th (C#), 9th (E), 11th (G), 13th (B)

Online access
flametreemusic.com

Scan the code
to hear the chord

D#/E♭
Major

Chord Spelling

1st (E♭), 3rd (G), 5th (B♭)

Online access
flametreemusic.com

Scan the code
to hear the chord

D#/E♭m
Minor

Chord Spelling

1st (E♭), ♭3rd (G♭), 5th (B♭)

D♯/E♭+
Augmented Triad

Chord Spelling
1st (E♭), 3rd (G), ♯5th (B)

Online access
flametreemusic.com

Scan the code
to hear the chord

D#/Eb°
Diminished Triad

Chord Spelling
1st (Eb), b3rd (Gb), b5th (Bbb)

Online access
flametreemusic.com

Scan the code
to hear the chord

D♯/E♭sus2
Suspended 2nd

Chord Spelling
1st (E♭), 2nd (F), 5th (B♭)

Online access
flametreemusic.com

Scan the code
to hear the chord

D♯/E♭sus4
Suspended 4th

Chord Spelling
1st (E♭), 4th (A♭), 5th (B♭)

Online access
flametreemusic.com Scan the code
to hear the chord

D#/E♭5
5th (Power Chord)

2

Chord Spelling
1st (E♭), 5th (B♭)

Online access
flametreemusic.com

Scan the code
to hear the chord

D♯/E♭6
Major 6th

Chord Spelling
1st (E♭), 3rd (G), 5th (B♭), 6th (C)

D#/E♭m6
Minor 6th

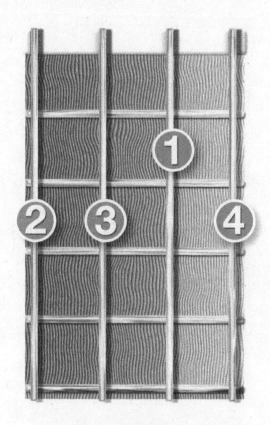

Chord Spelling
1st (E♭), ♭3rd (G♭), 5th (B♭), 6th (C)

D♯/E♭6sus4
6th Suspended 4th

Chord Spelling
1st (E♭), 4th (A♭), 5th (B♭), 6th (C)

Online access
flametreemusic.com

Scan the code
to hear the chord

D♯/E♭maj7
Major 7th

Chord Spelling
1st (E♭), 3rd (G), 5th (B♭), 7th (D)

D#/E♭m7
Minor 7th

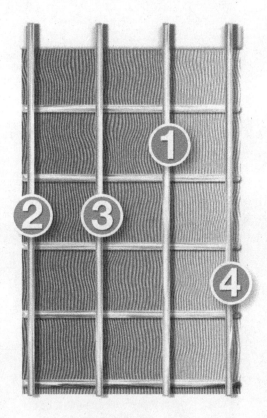

Chord Spelling
1st (E♭), ♭3rd (G♭), 5th (B♭), ♭7th (D♭)

Online access
flametreemusic.com

Scan the code
to hear the chord

D#/E♭7
Dominant 7th

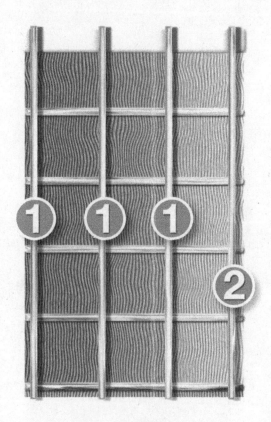

Chord Spelling
1st (E♭), 3rd (G), 5th (B♭), ♭7th (D♭)

Online access
flametreemusic.com Scan the code
to hear the chord

D♯/E♭°7
Diminished 7th

Chord Spelling

1st (E♭), ♭3rd (G♭), ♭5th (B♭♭), ♭♭7th (D♭♭)

Online access
flametreemusic.com

Scan the code
to hear the chord

D♯/E♭7sus4
Dominant 7th Suspended 4th

Chord Spelling
1st (E♭), 4th (A♭), 5th (B♭), ♭7th (D♭)

Online access
flametreemusic.com

Scan the code
to hear the chord

D#/E♭maj9
Major 9th

Chord Spelling
1st (E♭), 3rd (G), 5th (B♭), 7th (D), 9th (F)

Online access
flametreemusic.com

Scan the code
to hear the chord

D♯/E♭m9
Minor 9th

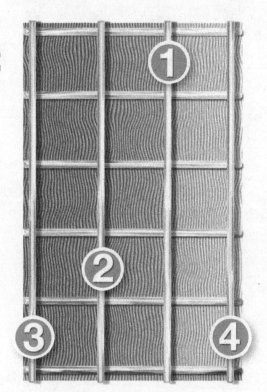

Chord Spelling
1st (E♭), ♭3rd (G♭), 5th (B♭), ♭7th (D♭), 9th (F)

Online access
flametreemusic.com

Scan the code
to hear the chord

D♯/E♭9
Dominant 9th

Chord Spelling

1st (E♭), 3rd (G), 5th (B♭), ♭7th (D♭), 9th (F)

D#/E♭maj11
Major 11th

Chord Spelling
1st (E♭), 3rd (G), 5th (B♭), 7th (D), 9th (F), 11th (A♭)

D♯/E♭maj13
Major 13th

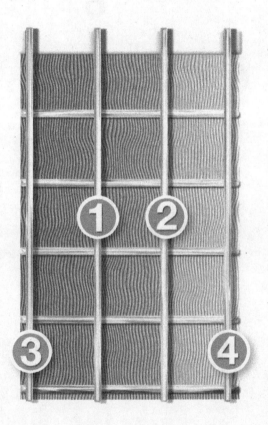

Chord Spelling

1st (E♭), 3rd (G), 5th (B♭), 7th (D), 9th (F), 11th (A♭), 13th (C)

Online access
flametreemusic.com

Scan the code
to hear the chord

E
Major

Chord Spelling
1st (E), 3rd (G#), 5th (B)

Online access
flametreemusic.com Scan the code
to hear the chord

Em
Minor

O

Chord Spelling
1st (E), ♭3rd (G), 5th (B)

E+
Augmented Triad

Chord Spelling
1st (E), 3rd (G#), #5th (B#)

Online access
flametreemusic.com

Scan the code
to hear the chord

E°
Diminished Triad

Chord Spelling
1st (E), ♭3rd (G), ♭5th (B♭)

Esus2
Suspended 2nd

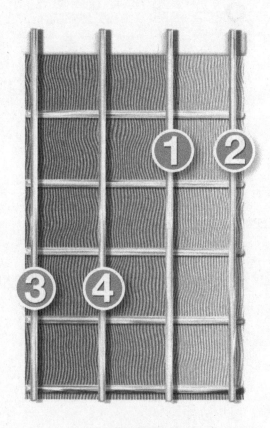

Chord Spelling
1st (E), 2nd (F#), 5th (B)

Online access
flametreemusic.com Scan the code
to hear the chord

Esus4
Suspended 4th

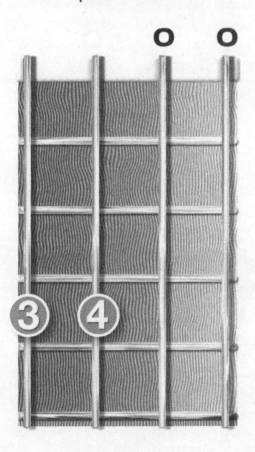

Chord Spelling
1st (E), 4th (A), 5th (B)

Online access
flametreemusic.com

Scan the code
to hear the chord

E5
5th (Power Chord)

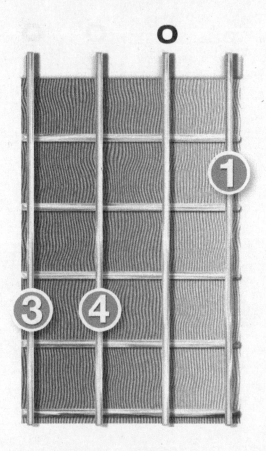

Chord Spelling
1st (E), 5th (B)

Online access
flametreemusic.com

Scan the code
to hear the chord

E6
Major 6th

Chord Spelling
1st (E), 3rd (G#), 5th (B), 6th (C#)

Em6
Minor 6th

Chord Spelling
1st (E), ♭3rd (G), 5th (B), 6th (C♯)

Online access
flametreemusic.com

Scan the code
to hear the chord

E6sus4
6th Suspended 4th

Chord Spelling
1st (D), 4th (G), 5th (A), 6th (B)

Online access
flametreemusic.com Scan the code
to hear the chord

Emaj7
Major 7th

Chord Spelling
1st (E), 3rd (G#), 5th (B), 7th (D#)

Online access
flametreemusic.com

Scan the code
to hear the chord

Em7
Minor 7th

Chord Spelling

1st (E), ♭3rd (G), 5th (B), ♭7th (D)

Online access
flametreemusic.com

Scan the code
to hear the chord

E7
Dominant 7th

Chord Spelling
1st (E), 3rd (G♯), 5th (B), ♭7th (D)

Online access
flametreemusic.com

Scan the code
to hear the chord

E°7
Diminished 7th

Chord Spelling

1st (E), ♭3rd (G), ♭5th (B♭), ♭♭7th (D♭)

Online access
flametreemusic.com

Scan the code
to hear the chord

E7sus4
Dominant 7th Suspended 4th

Chord Spelling
1st (D), 4th (G), 5th (A), ♭7th (C)

Online access
flametreemusic.com Scan the code
to hear the chord

Emaj9
Major 9th

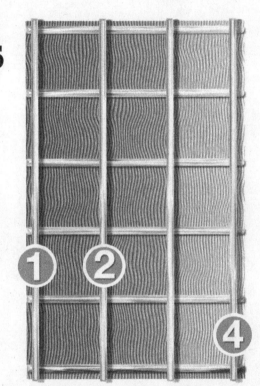

Chord Spelling
1st (E), 3rd (G#), 5th (B), 7th (D#), 9th (F#)

Online access
flametreemusic.com

Scan the code
to hear the chord

Em9
Minor 9th

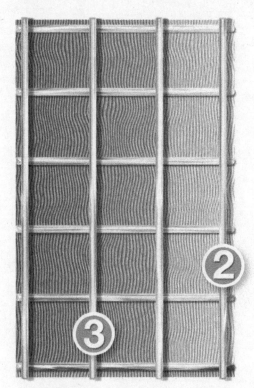

Chord Spelling
1st (E), ♭3rd (G), 5th (B), ♭7th (D), 9th (F♯)

Online access
flametreemusic.com

Scan the code
to hear the chord

E9
Dominant 9th

3

Chord Spelling

1st (E), 3rd (G♯), 5th (B), ♭7th (D), 9th (F♯)

Online access
flametreemusic.com

Scan the code
to hear the chord

Emaj11
Major 11th

Chord Spelling
1st (E), 3rd (G♯), 5th (B), 7th (D♯), 9th (F♯), 11th (A)

Online access
flametreemusic.com

Scan the code
to hear the chord

Emaj13
Major 13th

Chord Spelling

1st (E), 3rd (G#), 5th (B), 7th (D#), 9th (F), 11th (A), 13th (C#)

Online access
flametreemusic.com

Scan the code
to hear the chord

175

F
Major

Chord Spelling
1st (F), 3rd (A), 5th (C)

Online access
flametreemusic.com Scan the code
to hear the chord

Fm
Minor

Chord Spelling

1st (F), ♭3rd (A♭), 5th (C)

Online access
flametreemusic.com

Scan the code
to hear the chord

F+
Augmented Triad

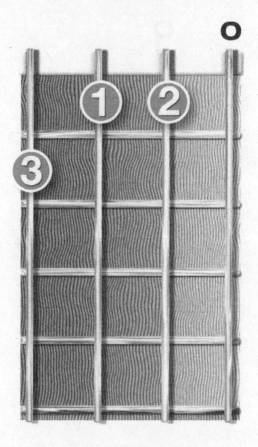

Chord Spelling
1st (F), 3rd (A), #5th (C#)

Online access
flametreemusic.com

Scan the code
to hear the chord

F°
Diminished Triad

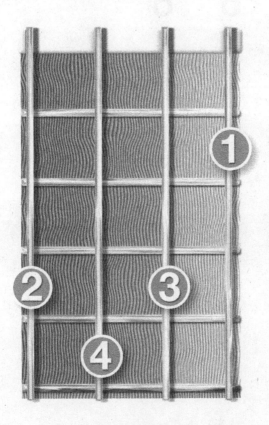

Chord Spelling
1st (F), ♭3rd (A♭), ♭5th (C♭)

Fsus2
Suspended 2nd

Chord Spelling
1st (F), 2nd (G), 5th (C)

Online access
flametreemusic.com

Scan the code
to hear the chord

Fsus4
Suspended 4th

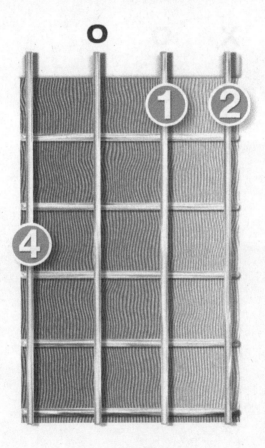

Chord Spelling
1st (F), 4th (B♭), 5th (C)

Online access
flametreemusic.com

Scan the code
to hear the chord

F5
5th (Power Chord)

Chord Spelling
1st (F), 5th (C)

Online access
flametreemusic.com Scan the code
to hear the chord

F6
Major 6th

Chord Spelling
1st (F), 3rd (A), 5th (C), 6th (D)

Online access
flametreemusic.com

Scan the code
to hear the chord

Fm6
Minor 6th

Chord Spelling
1st (F), ♭3rd (A♭), 5th (C), 6th (D)

F6sus4
6th Suspended 4th

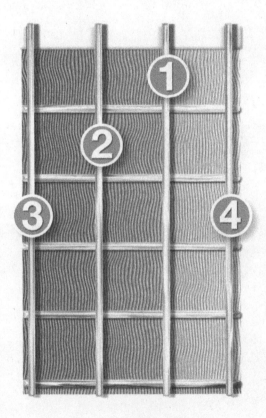

Chord Spelling
1st (F), 4th (B♭), 5th (C), 6th (D)

Online access
flametreemusic.com Scan the code
to hear the chord

Fmaj7
Major 7th

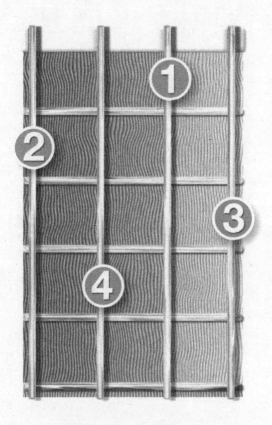

Chord Spelling
1st (F), 3rd (A), 5th (C), 7th (E)

Fm7
Minor 7th

Chord Spelling
1st (F), ♭3rd (A♭), 5th (C), ♭7th (E♭)

F7
Dominant 7th

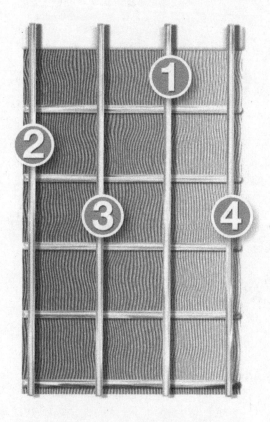

Chord Spelling

1st (F), 3rd (A), 5th (C), ♭7th (E♭)

F°7
Diminished 7th

Chord Spelling

1st (F), ♭3rd (A♭), ♭5th (C♭), ♭♭7th (E♭♭)

Online access
flametreemusic.com

Scan the code
to hear the chord

F7sus4
Dominant 7th Suspended 4th

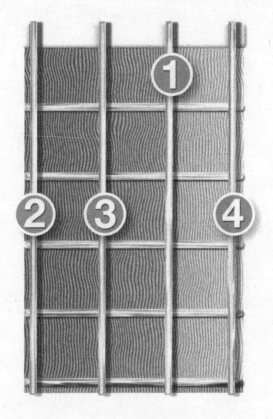

Chord Spelling
1st (F), 4th (B♭), 5th (C), ♭7th (E♭)

Online access
flametreemusic.com

Scan the code
to hear the chord

Fmaj9
Major 9th

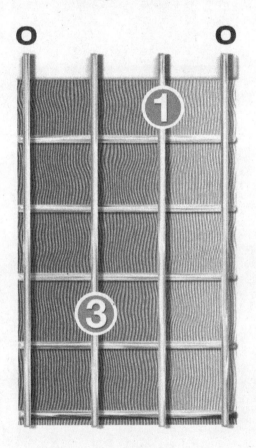

Chord Spelling
1st (F), 3rd (A), 5th (C), 7th (E), 9th (G)

Online access
flametreemusic.com

Scan the code
to hear the chord

Fm9
Minor 9th

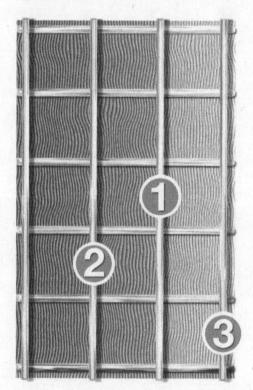

Chord Spelling
1st (F#), ♭3rd (A), 5th (C#), ♭7th (E), 9th (G#)

Online access
flametreemusic.com

Scan the code
to hear the chord

F9
Dominant 9th

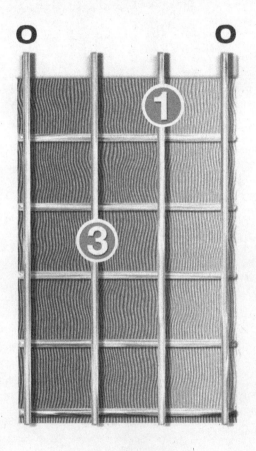

Chord Spelling
1st (F), 3rd (A), 5th (C), ♭7th (E♭), 9th (G)

Fmaj11
Major 11th

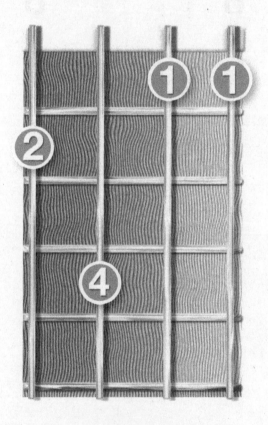

Chord Spelling

1st (F), 3rd (A), 5th (C), 7th (E), 9th (G), 11th (B♭)

Online access
flametreemusic.com

Scan the code
to hear the chord

Fmaj13
Major 13th

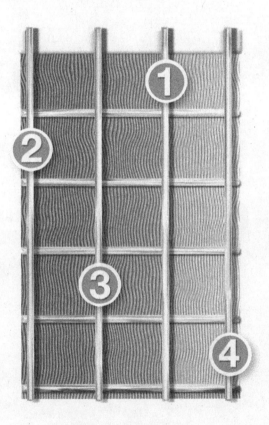

Chord Spelling

1st (F), 3rd (A), 5th (C), 7th (E), 9th (G), 11th (B♭), 13th (D)

Online access
flametreemusic.com Scan the code
to hear the chord

195

F♯/G♭
Major

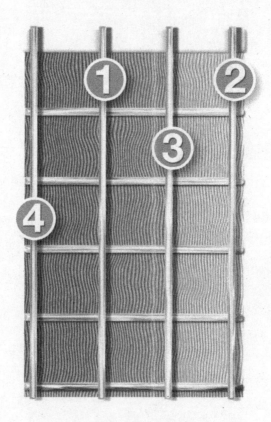

Chord Spelling
1st (F♯), 3rd (A♯), 5th (C♯)

F#/G♭m
Minor

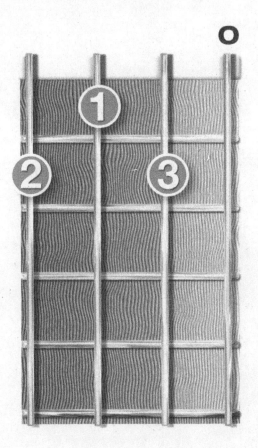

Chord Spelling
1st (F#), ♭3rd (A), 5th (C#)

Online access
flametreemusic.com

Scan the code
to hear the chord

F♯/G♭+
Augmented Triad

Chord Spelling
1st (F♯), 3rd (A♯), ♯5th (Cx)

Online access
flametreemusic.com

Scan the code
to hear the chord

F♯/G♭°
Diminished Triad

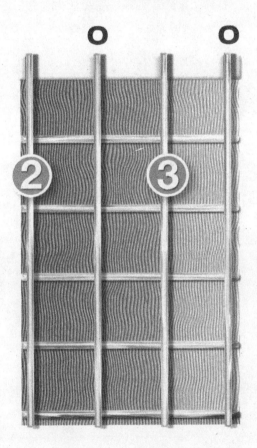

Chord Spelling
1st (F♯), ♭3rd (A), ♭5th (C)

Online access
flametreemusic.com

Scan the code
to hear the chord

F#/G♭sus2
Suspended 2nd

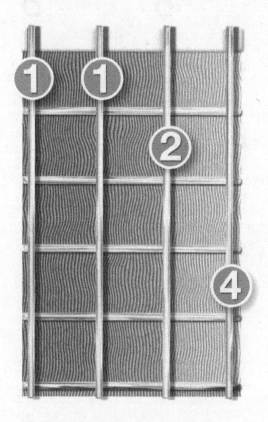

Chord Spelling
1st (F#), 2nd (G#), 5th (C#)

F#/G♭sus4
Suspended 4th

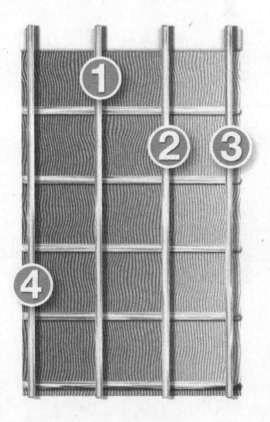

Chord Spelling
1st (F#), 4th (B), 5th (C#)

Online access
flametreemusic.com

Scan the code
to hear the chord

F#/Gb5
5th (Power Chord)

X

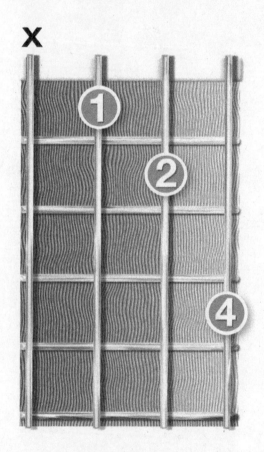

Chord Spelling
1st (F#), 5th (C#)

Online access
flametreemusic.com

Scan the code
to hear the chord

F♯/G♭6
Major 6th

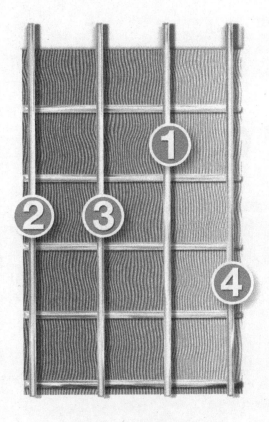

Chord Spelling
1st (F♯), 3rd (A♯), 5th (C♯), 6th (D♯)

F#/G♭m6
Minor 6th

Chord Spelling
1st (F#), ♭3rd (A), 5th (C#), 6th (D#)

F#/G♭6sus4
6th Suspended 4th

Chord Spelling

1st (F#), 4th (B), 5th (C#), 6th (D#)

F#/G♭maj7
Major 7th

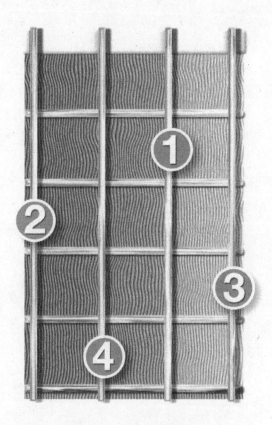

Chord Spelling
1st (F#), 3rd (A#), 5th (C#), 7th (F)

F♯/G♭m7
Minor 7th

Chord Spelling
1st (F♯), ♭3rd (A), 5th (C♯), ♭7th (E)

F#/G♭7
Dominant 7th

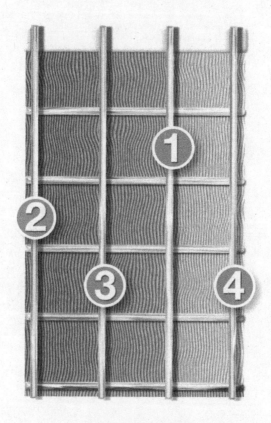

Chord Spelling
1st (F#), 3rd (A#), 5th (C#), ♭7th (E)

F♯/G♭°7
Diminished 7th

Chord Spelling
1st (F♯), ♭3rd (A), ♭5th (C), ♭♭7th (E♭)

F♯/G♭7sus4
Dominant 7th Suspended 4th

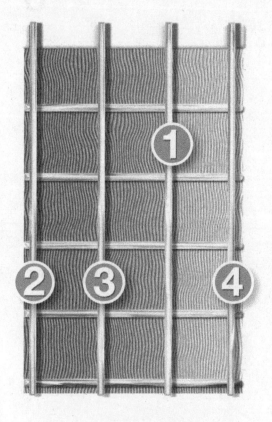

Chord Spelling
1st (F♯), 4th (B), 5th (C♯), ♭7th (E)

Online access
flametreemusic.com

Scan the code
to hear the chord

F#/G♭maj9
Major 9th

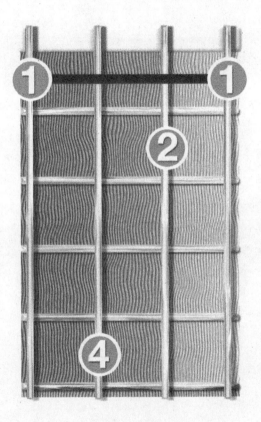

Chord Spelling
1st (F#), 3rd (A#), 5th (C#), 7th (E#), 9th (G#)

Online access
flametreemusic.com

Scan the code
to hear the chord

F#/G♭m9
Minor 9th

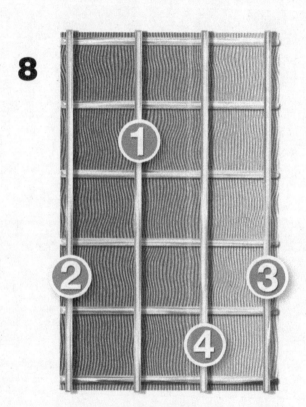

8

Chord Spelling
1st (F#), ♭3rd (A), 5th (C#), ♭7th (E), 9th (G#)

F♯/G♭9
Dominant 9th

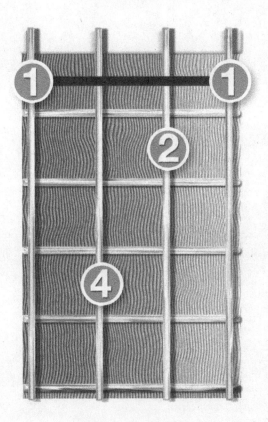

Chord Spelling
1st (F♯), 3rd (A♯), 5th (C♯), ♭7th (E), 9th (G♯)

F#/Gbmaj11
Major 11th

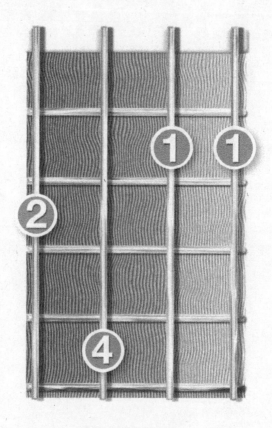

Chord Spelling
1st (F#), 3rd (A#), 5th (C#), 7th (E#), 9th (G#), 11th (B)

F♯/G♭maj13
Major 13th

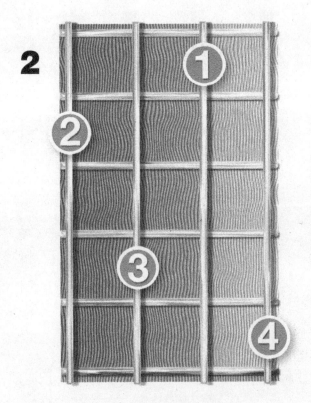

Chord Spelling
1st (F♯), 3rd (A♯), 5th (C♯), 7th (E♯), 9th (G♯), 11th (B), 13th (D♯)

Online access
flametreemusic.com

Scan the code
to hear the chord

G
Major

Chord Spelling
1st (G), 3rd (B), 5th (D)

Online access
flametreemusic.com

Scan the code
to hear the chord

Gm
Minor

Chord Spelling
1st (G), ♭3rd (B♭), 5th (D)

Online access
flametreemusic.com Scan the code
to hear the chord

G+
Augmented Triad

Chord Spelling
1st (G), 3rd (B), #5th (D#)

G°
Diminished Triad

Chord Spelling
1st (G), ♭3rd (B♭), ♭5th (D♭)

Gsus2
Suspended 2nd

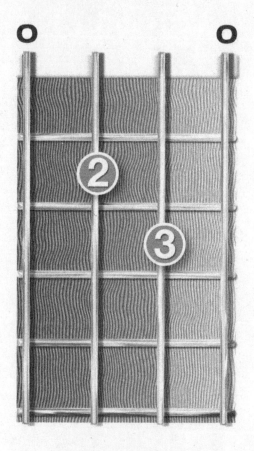

Chord Spelling
1st (G), 2nd (A), 5th (D)

Online access
flametreemusic.com

Scan the code
to hear the chord

Gsus4
Suspended 4th

Chord Spelling
1st (G), 4th (C), 5th (D)

Online access
flametreemusic.com

Scan the code
to hear the chord

G5
5th (Power Chord)

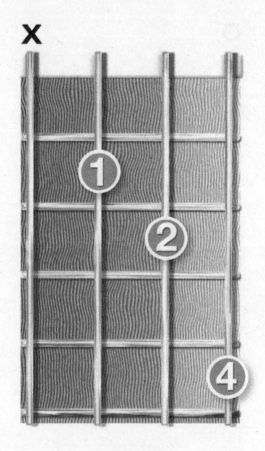

Chord Spelling
1st (G), 5th (D)

Online access
flametreemusic.com

Scan the code
to hear the chord

G6
Major 6th

Chord Spelling
1st (G), 3rd (B), 5th (D), 6th (E)

Online access
flametreemusic.com

Scan the code
to hear the chord

Gm6
Minor 6th

Chord Spelling
1st (G), ♭3rd (B♭), 5th (D), 6th (E)

G6sus4
6th Suspended 4th

Chord Spelling
1st (G), 4th (C), 5th (D), 6th (E)

Online access
flametreemusic.com

Scan the code
to hear the chord

Gmaj7
Major 7th

Chord Spelling
1st (G), 3rd (B), 5th (D), 7th (F#)

Online access
flametreemusic.com

Scan the code
to hear the chord

Gm7
Minor 7th

Chord Spelling
1st (G), ♭3rd (B♭), 5th (D), ♭7th (F)

Online access
flametreemusic.com

Scan the code
to hear the chord

G7
Dominant 7th

Chord Spelling
1st (G), 3rd (B), 5th (D), ♭7th (F)

G°7
Diminished 7th

Chord Spelling
1st (G), ♭3rd (B♭), ♭5th (D♭), ♭♭7th (F♭)

G7sus4
Dominant 7th Suspended 4th

Chord Spelling
1st (G), 4th (C), 5th (D), ♭7th (F)

Gmaj9
Major 9th

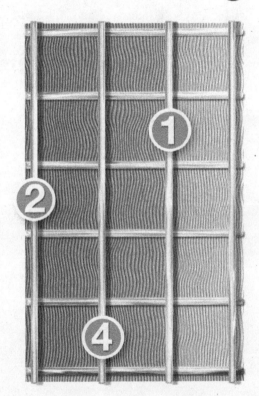

Chord Spelling
1st (G), 3rd (B), 5th (D), 7th (F#), 9th (A)

Gm9
Minor 9th

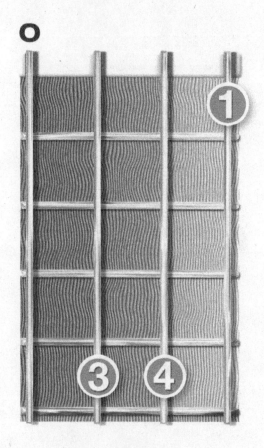

Chord Spelling
1st (G), ♭3rd (B♭), 5th (D), ♭7th (F), 9th (A)

Online access
flametreemusic.com

Scan the code
to hear the chord

G9
Dominant 9th

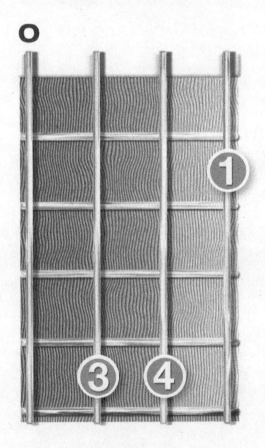

Chord Spelling
1st (G), 3rd (B), 5th (D), ♭7th (F), 9th (A)

Gmaj11
Major 11th

Chord Spelling
1st (G), 3rd (B), 5th (D), 7th (F#), 9th (A), 11th (C)

Online access
flametreemusic.com

Scan the code
to hear the chord

Gmaj13
Major 13th

Chord Spelling

1st (G), 3rd (B), 5th (D), 7th (F♯), 9th (A), 11th (C), 13th (E)

G♯/A♭
Major

Chord Spelling
1st (A♭), 3rd (C), 5th (E♭)

G#/A♭m
Minor

Chord Spelling
1st (A♭), ♭3rd (C♭), 5th (E♭)

G#/A♭+
Augmented Triad

Chord Spelling
1st (A♭), 3rd (C), #5th (E)

Online access
flametreemusic.com

Scan the code
to hear the chord

G#/A♭°
Diminished Triad

Chord Spelling
1st (A♭), ♭3rd (C♭), ♭5th (E♭♭)

G♯/A♭sus2
Suspended 2nd

Chord Spelling
1st (A♭), 2nd (B♭), 5th (E♭)

G#/A♭sus4
Suspended 4th

Chord Spelling
1st (A♭), 4th (D♭), 5th (E♭)

Online access
flametreemusic.com

Scan the code
to hear the chord

G#/A♭5
5th (Power Chord)

X

Chord Spelling
1st (A♭), 5th (E♭)

G#/A♭6
Major 6th

Chord Spelling
1st (A♭), 3rd (C), 5th (E♭), 6th (F)

Online access
flametreemusic.com

Scan the code
to hear the chord

G♯/A♭m6
Minor 6th

Chord Spelling
1st (A♭), ♭3rd (C♭), 5th (E♭), 6th (F)

G#/A♭6sus4
6th Suspended 4th

Chord Spelling
1st (A♭), 4th (D♭), 5th (E♭), 6th (F)

G#/A♭maj7
Major 7th

Chord Spelling
1st (A♭), 3rd (C), 5th (E♭), 7th (G)

Online access
flametreemusic.com

Scan the code
to hear the chord

G#/Abm7
Minor 7th

Chord Spelling
1st (Ab), b3rd (Cb), 5th (Eb), b7th (Gb)

G#/A♭7
Dominant 7th

Chord Spelling
1st (A♭), 3rd (C), 5th (E♭), ♭7th (G♭)

G♯/A♭°7
Diminished 7th

Chord Spelling
1st (A♭), ♭3rd (C♭), ♭5th (E♭♭), ♭♭7th (G♭♭)

G#/Ab7sus4
Dominant 7th Suspended 4th

Chord Spelling
1st (Ab), 4th (Db), 5th (Eb), b7th (Gb)

G#/A♭maj9
Major 9th

Chord Spelling
1st (A♭), 3rd (C), 5th (E♭), 7th (G), 9th (B♭)

Online access
flametreemusic.com

Scan the code
to hear the chord

G#/A♭m9
Minor 9th

7

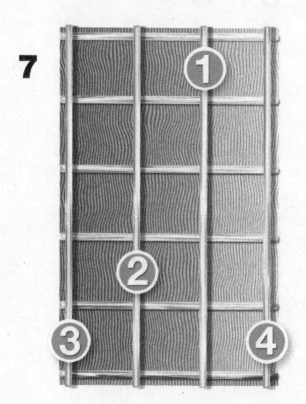

Chord Spelling
1st (A♭), ♭3rd (C♭), 5th (E♭), ♭7th (G♭), 9th (B♭)

G#/Ab9
Dominant 9th

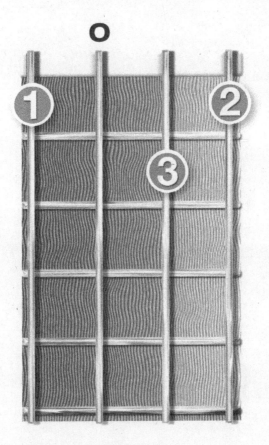

Chord Spelling
1st (Ab), 3rd (C), 5th (Eb), b7th (Gb), 9th (Bb)

Online access
flametreemusic.com

Scan the code
to hear the chord

G#/A♭maj11
Major 11th

Chord Spelling
1st (A♭), 3rd (C), 5th (E♭), 7th (G), 9th (B♭), 11th (D♭)

Online access
flametreemusic.com

Scan the code
to hear the chord

G#/A♭maj13
Major 13th

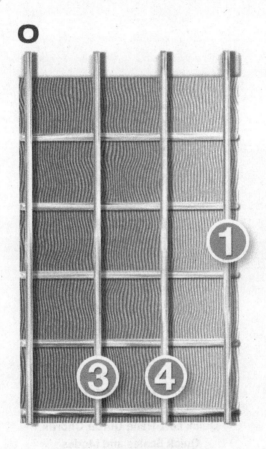

Chord Spelling

1st (A♭), 3rd (C), 5th (B♭), 7th (G), 9th (B♭), 11th (D♭), 13th (F)

Online access
flametreemusic.com

Scan the code
to hear the chord

SEE, LISTEN, LEARN
Make it Your Own

See our books, journals,
notebooks & calendars at
flametreepublishing.com

•

Books in this series:
Quick Piano & Keyboard Chords
Quick Guitar Chords
Quick Left-Hand Guitar Chords
Quick Scales and Modes
Quick How to Read Music